First published in the United States by
The Lighthouse Academy Press
Printed by Kindle Direct Publishing, USA
Additional copies for sale at Amazon Books

ISBN: 979-8-9995192-1-4

This work was created through a human–AI collaboration. Drafts of text, arrangement, and information were generated using advanced AI tools. The author then restructured sections and reviewed, revised, and refined all text for adherence to intent, coherence, and literary voice. See *Author's Note.*

Walking the Porch

*A Stoic's Guide
for the Curious Traveler*

by

William J. Striker

Contents

Preface

Let us be honest with one another at the outset.

If you're holding this book, you're likely a seeker. Not of quotes, but of clarity. Not of inspiration, but of integration. You've heard of Stoicism—perhaps in passing, perhaps in pain—and you want to know what it *really* is.

What you've found so far is probably one of two things:

- **The Academic Obelisk**: A towering mass of footnotes, Latin phrases, and arguments over whether Cleanthes really meant *logos* or *Logos*. A book that explains every angle of the Stoic pin—but never shows you what it's for.

- **The Influencer's Soapbox**: Dressed in modern slang, punctuated with "inspirational" quotes, these books often drip with the insecurity of someone who read Marcus Aurelius once, took a cold shower, and decided they were qualified to teach *virtue*. What follows is not Stoicism—it's self-help cosplay with borrowed gravitas.

Both are forms of vanity. One hides behind ivory walls; the other hides behind ring lights. Neither helps the traveler walk a path that grounds her or him.

This book is neither.

It is a **field manual**, a **tourist guide**, a **companion for the curious and philosophically serious**— those who do not want to *become* Seneca or Epictetus, but who want to walk beside them long enough to hear what they're really saying. There is no attempt here to fill the role of a sage, nor even to know the terrain beyond general directions.

Stoicism deserves better than to be embalmed in academia or pimped out by charlatans. It was a living, breathing system designed to teach people how to live well, suffer well, and die well. It did not demand perfection. It demanded effort. Not brilliance—but honesty.

This book is written in that spirit. You'll find here a simple principle:

**Don't read the guy talking about the guy.
Read the guy.**

This guide is here to help do exactly that—with context only where needed. Not as a modern voice pretending to be ancient, but as a traveler pointing toward a path.

You will find no posturing here. No pageantry. No AI trying to pretend it's human—and no human trying to pretend he's Epictetus. Just a collaboration of one man and one machine, both devoted to helping you figure out for *yourself* what the Stoics were really getting at, and how you might bring that into your own life, one choice at a time, on your terms.

—WJS

Walking the Porch

*A Stoic's Guide
for the Curious Traveler*

The Arc of Stoicism

Stoicism was never static. It moved, breathed, and aged—its tone shifting with the times, its clarity tested by empires, slavery, corruption, and war. The heart remained, but the voices changed. Understanding them is not an academic exercise—it is a way to locate the present moment within a lineage of thought that has always been about action.

Introduction
On the Porch

This book is named for a place—the **Stoa Poikile**, or "Painted Porch," in ancient Athens. It was there that Zeno of Citium began teaching what would become known as Stoicism. He taught not from a platform or pulpit, but in the open, in motion, among the people. It was philosophy in the world, not apart from it. No robes. No incense. Just questions, clarity, and the hard work of becoming free. Zeno's followers were known as **Stoikoi** ("porch people").

To "walk the Porch" today is to pick up that tradition—not as a scholar preserving artifacts, and not as a preacher selling life hacks—but as a traveler looking for a reliable compass.

The Porch is not a destination or a place to pass the time away. It is a threshold. A place to step out of the noise, take in the wider view, and prepare to reenter the world with a steadier footing.

This book is a **field guide**. It does not offer a system, a certification, or a new identity. It offers orientation—so that when the world rattles your soul (as it will), you'll have something older and steadier to reach for.

Before you begin, it may help to understand the background, precepts, and lineage of Stoic voices.

The Stoa Poikile (c. 430 BC)

A long, open-fronted colonnade, with a solid back wall and a shallow roof, freestanding along the north edge of the Agora.

Artist's reconstruction based on archaeological remains from the Athenian Agora, Roman-era architectural fragments, and ancient written accounts, including Pausanias and Diogenes Laërtius.

This image reflects how the Painted Porch may have appeared in the early Classical period, shortly after its construction. The Doric colonnade fronted a shaded promenade lined with large panel paintings and war trophies—serving as a civic, artistic, and philosophical gathering place.

It was here that Zeno of Citium began teaching Stoic philosophy over 2,300 years ago, giving Stoicism its name.

Core Stoic Concepts

A brief guide to the language of the Porch

Virtue

The only true good. Not a single trait, but the harmony of reason, courage, justice, and self-control. The Stoic does not pursue happiness. The Stoic pursues virtue—and finds *freedom* there.

Logos

The rational order of the universe. Not a god with a face, but a structure with meaning. The task of the Stoic is to live in agreement with it.

Nature

Not nature as scenery, but nature as reality—*what is*. The Stoic seeks to live not in rebellion against life, but in accordance with its terms.

Externals

All things beyond your control: your body, reputation, wealth, health, outcomes, and the actions of others. These are not evil—but they are *not yours*.

The Dichotomy of Control

Some things are up to you. Some are not. Wisdom begins by making this distinction—and peace comes from staying on your side of the line.

The Passions

Destructive emotions born from mistaken

judgments. Anger, fear, envy, anxiety—they arise when you expect the world to obey you.

The Sage

A rare, perhaps impossible ideal: the person who *lives completely by reason*. The Stoic does not need to become the sage—only to walk in that direction.

Before the Porch:
The Threads Leading to Stoicism

Philosophy didn't begin with the Stoics. They built on something older. Before the Porch was raised, Socrates stood in the street, asking uncomfortable questions. His life was a fire that illuminated the way forward—and the Stoics never forgot him.

He gathered four threads from the thinkers before him:

1. **Nature** — from Heraclitus and others who sought to understand the world as a system of charge and order.

2. **Reason** — from the Eleatics and Pythagoreans, who searched for what was eternal and knowable.

3. **Virtue** — from poets and tragedians, who wrestled with what it meant to act rightly, even when doomed.

4. **The Soul** — from mystery cults, Orphics, and early moral reflection: the idea that who you are is more than what you have.

Socrates did something radical with these threads. He tied them to daily life. He made **ethics the center of philosophy**—and lived it to the end.

<u>What Socrates Gave the Stoics</u>

1. Virtue Is the Only Good

Socrates claimed that a person who *knows* the good will *do* the good, and that no harm can befall a good soul. This is directly echoed by Epictetus and cleanly mapped in Stoic doctrine.

Epictetus:

> *"No one can harm you unless you harm yourself."*

2. Living in Accordance with Reason

Socrates believed the rational soul was the highest part of man. The Stoics formalized this as living in accordance with Logos—the reason in the universe and within the individual.

3. Self-Scrutiny and Ethical Examination

> *"The unexamined life is not worth living."*

This is the very spirit of Stoic journaling (Marcus), moral self-auditing (Seneca), and daily philosophical training (Epictetus).

4. Public Integrity over Personal Gain

Socrates' refusal to compromise in court—choosing death rather than violating principle—was Stoicism incarnate before the name existed.

Marcus, Epictetus, and Seneca all viewed this act not as tragedy, but as triumph.

The Stoics took his marble blocks and built the Porch.

Socrates
(c. 470–399 BC)

Traditional Roman-era depiction of the Athenian philosopher. Based on marble busts housed in the Louvre and other collections.

Early Stoics:
Power of Virtue

In the Early Stoa (Zeno, Cleanthes, Chrysippus), Stoicism was robust, confident, and systematizing. These were builders and visionaries, proclaiming:

- The universe is rational

- Virtue is the only good

- Wisdom allows harmony with Nature and Logos

It was Herculean, almost Promethean in tone—a cosmic optimism about the human capacity for reason and self-mastery. Think of the early Stoics as the architects of the Temple of Virtue.

What is Logos?

In Stoic thought, logos is the rational structure that underlies the universe—a kind of living logic.
To the Stoics, it is not a god in human form, but a sacred order—a living logic.
To live in harmony with Logos is to live with clarity, courage, and acceptance of what is.

Zeno of Citium
(c. 334–262 BC)

Traditional Roman-era depiction of the founder of Stoicism. Based on sculptural references housed in the Pushkin Museum and other classical collections.

Seneca:
The Noble Patrician
Wrestling with Power

Seneca (c. 4 BC – AD 65), writing in the heart of Nero's Rome, embodies dignity under pressure. He writes as a man in the halls of power who knows the abyss is close:

- His prose is elegant, polished, Roman

- He teaches how to survive morally in a corrupt world

- He shows how far one can bend before breaking

Seneca is not yet tired, but he's compromised—an idealist with blood on his toga. One foot in the palace, one in the grave. He represents the transitional energy: still grand, but wavering.

Peak energy? If measured by cultural influence and literary brilliance—yes, perhaps it is Seneca. But if measured by philosophical fire, another voice rises.

Seneca the Younger
(c.4 BC–AD 65)
Artist's interpretation inspired
by the Roman double-herm
bust housed in the Altes
Museum, Berlin. Considered
the most historically accurate
likeness of the Stoic
philosopher, this
representation reflects
Seneca's weathered presence
here reflects the burden of
living with clarity under a
reign that rewarded silence
and punished virtue.

Epictetus:
The Burning Core

Epictetus (c. AD 55 – 135) is the clearest voice of
Stoic fire and focus:

- Born a slave. Disabled. Freed. He owned
  nothing—except his mind.

- He stripped Stoicism to its bare essentials:
  what is in your control, and what is not.

- He taught not to debate virtue but to live it.
  No excuses.

There's an austerity to him—bracing, pure, and
uncompromising. No marble statues. No quoting the
poets. Just: *Do not be disturbed.* Live by reason. Be free,
even if chained.

Yes, Epictetus may be considered the energetic apex
of Stoicism's inner revolution.

His words have fueled Christians, Enlightenment
philosophers, soldiers, and strugglers for centuries.
He is not a relic—he is the lit flame.

Epictetus
(c.AD 55–135)

No authenticated ancient bust survives. This is a widely accepted traditional representation.

Marcus Aurelius:
The Stoic Sunset

Marcus (AD 121–180) writes in the shadow of empire's decline. He is a good man carrying a collapsing world:

- Meditations is a personal journal, not a public doctrine

- It is full of resignation, fatigue, and a longing for rest

- Still committed—but always on the brink of despair

His Stoicism is beautiful, reflective, but exhausted. It is the sound of a man holding the moral line alone in the night.

Marcus Aurelius
(AD 121–180)

Roman emperor and Stoic philosopher. This depiction is inspired by numerous surviving marble busts, including those housed in the Capitoline Museums and the Glyptothek in Munich. His reign marked the final flowering of classical Stoicism, written amidst war, duty, and decline.

Stoic Voices
Referenced in This Guide

A brief guide to the writings of those who speak in these pages

Marcus Aurelius (AD 121–180)

- *Meditations* — A personal journal written by a Roman emperor in the midst of war, duty, and loss. Reflective, weary, steady.

Epictetus (c. AD 55–135)

- *Discourses* — Recorded by his student Arrian, these lectures teach the practical work of Stoic discipline.

- *Enchiridion* (The Handbook) — A short manual of Stoic clarity, written for daily use.

Seneca (c. 4 BC – AD 65)

- *Letters to Lucilius* — 124 letters to a younger friend, written with rhetorical beauty and moral force.

- Selected Essays — *On the Shortness of Life, On Anger, On Tranquility of Mind,* and others. Stoicism in the palace and on the edge of death.

Musonius Rufus (1st century AD)

- *Lectures and Sayings* — Practical teachings on simplicity, discipline, and moral training. Partial fragments survive.

Others Quoted Indirectly

- *Zeno of Citium, Cleanthes, Chrysippus, Panaetius, Hierocles* — Early and Middle Stoics whose ideas survive through fragments and later writers. Their voices shape the background of the Porch.

Pre-Stoic Reading

Voices that shaped the Stoic world before it had a name

Socrates (c. 470–399 BC)

– No writings of his own survive, but his life and method appear in:

- Plato's *Dialogues* (esp. *Apology*, *Crito*, *Phaedo*)
- Xenophon's *Memorabilia*

Socrates brought philosophy into the streets. He shifted it from cosmic speculation to daily ethics. The Stoics saw him not as a predecessor—but as a model of the Sage.

Heraclitus (c. 535–475 BC)

– Fragmentary writings survive (often titled *Fragments*)
– Introduced the concept of **Logos** as a principle of order and change

His ideas fed directly into Stoic cosmology. Epictetus quotes him repeatedly.

Diogenes the Cynic (c. 412–323 BC)

– No writings survive, but sayings and stories are preserved
– His radical self-sufficiency and disdain for status deeply influenced early Stoics

Zeno, the Stoic founder, studied under Crates— himself a disciple of Diogenes.

Plato (c. 427–347 BC) and Aristotle (c. 384–322 BC)

– While not Stoics, their exploration of virtue, reason, and the soul set the stage
– Useful for understanding the moral climate the Stoics responded to

Orientation

Earlier Stoics exalted virtue as power—a kind of moral physics. Epictetus introduced the daily practice of that virtue—not as abstract philosophy, but as spiritual discipline. In this sense, he is both the peak and pivot of the tradition.

Marcus is the echo. A voice that reminds what can be salvaged when all else is lost.

The Porch remains open.

Energy & Voice of the Stoics

(A Comparative Summary)

Philosopher	Energy Level	Tone	Role in Stoicism
Zeno & Chrysippus	High	Constructive, bold	Founders & systematizers
Seneca	Fluctuating	Polished, anxious	Political survivalist, literary master
Epictetus	Sharp	Spartan, electric	Purifier and ethical drill instructor
Marcus Aurelius	Fading	Introspective, weary	Stoic king meditating in decline

Connections

- The **early Stoics (Zeno to Chrysippus)** were rooted in Athens, heavily influenced by Cynicism, Socratic ethics, and Heraclitean physics.

- **Middle Stoics** such as **Panaetius and Posidonius** increasingly blended **Platonic and Aristotelian** ideas, adapting to Roman tastes.

- **Roman Stoics (Seneca, Epictetus, Marcus)** emphasized **practical ethics** and personal integrity in public life and hardship.

- The **Cynics** (Antisthenes, Diogenes) pioneered radical self-sufficiency and moral clarity, prefiguring Stoic austerity.

- The **Academy** (founded by Plato), especially under **Xenocrates and Polemon**, focused on the **moral shaping of character**, which dovetailed into Zeno's early Stoicism.

<u>Key Stoic Philosophers</u>

Stoicism evolved over centuries, shaped by teachers, writers, and rulers. While many voices contributed, only a few left behind writings that still survive in full. Each belongs to a phase in the movement's arc: the bold architects, the Roman reformers, and the last voices before the Porch fell silent.

Stoic Philosophers			
Philosopher	Lifespan (Approx.)	Region	Notes
Zeno of Citium	334–262 BC	Citium, Cyprus	**Founder of Stoicism.** Taught at the Stoa Poikile in Athens.
Cleanthes	330–230 BC	Assos, Asia Minor	Disciple of Zeno, famous for *Hymn to Zeus* .
Chrysippus	280–206 BC	Soli, Cilicia (Asia Minor)	Systematizer of Stoicism. Expanded logic and ethics.
Diogenes of Babylon	c. 230–150 BC	Seleucia (Babylonia)	Brought Stoicism to Rome with Panaetius.
Antipater of Tarsus	d. c. 129 BC	Tarsus, Cilicia	Pupil of Diogenes of Babylon. Advanced ethics.
Panaetius	c. 185–110 BC	Rhodes	Blended Stoicism with Platonism and Aristotelianism.
Posidonius	c. 135–51 BC	Apamea, Syria	Polymath: ethics, astronomy, history. Student of Panaetius.
Cicero (not a Stoic)	106–43 BC	Arpinum, Italy	Popularized Stoicism in Latin, especially from Panaetius.
Seneca	c. 4 BC – AD 65	Corduba, Hispania	Roman Stoic, adviser to Nero. Famous for essays and letters.
Epictetus	c. AD 55 – 135	Hierapolis, Phrygia	Slave-turned-philosopher; his *Discourses* recorded by Arrian.
Marcus Aurelius	AD 121 – 180	Rome	Roman Emperor; *Meditations* is a Stoic classic.

Notable Pre-Stoic Personalities

Before Stoicism took form, many thinkers laid the groundwork—probing nature, reason, and the shape of a good life. The figures below represent the currents of philosophy that flowed into Socrates, and from him, into the Stoic tradition. They didn't speak with one voice, but together they stirred the questions Stoicism would later answer.

Notable Pre-Stoics			
Philosopher	Lifespan (Approx.)	Region	Notes
Socrates	470–399 BC	Athens	Moral exemplar for Stoics. Didn't write—known via Plato/Xenophon.
Plato	427–347 BC	Athens	Founded the Academy. Emphasized ideal forms, virtue, dialectic.
Xenocrates	396–314 BC	Chalcedon (Bithynia)	Successor to Plato; linked ethics to metaphysics.
Polemon of Athens	c. 350–270 BC	Athens	Head of the Academy; emphasized moral transformation.
Antisthenes	c. 445–365 BC	Athens	Socratic disciple, founder of the Cynic school.
Diogenes of Sinope	c. 412–323 BC	Sinope (Asia Minor)	Most famous Cynic. Radical simplicity, freedom from convention.
Heraclitus	c. 535–475 BC	Ephesus (Ionia)	Taught logos, flux, unity of opposites—deeply influenced Stoic physics.

Some Domains of Stoicism

Stoicism is not a system to be memorized. It is a way to meet life. These domains are not chapters in a doctrine—they are moments that test the soul: loss, fear, anger, illness, joy, and choice. Each section offers a brief reflection drawn from the voices of the Stoics themselves. This is not the full terrain, only part of it. But it is enough to begin.

1. What is Not Yours

---

*On control, externals, and
the foundation of Stoic freedom.*

"Some things are up to us, and some are not."
  —Epictetus, Enchiridion §1

This is **the beginning of all Stoic thought.**

There are things that belong to you: your judgments, your choices, your values.

There are things that do not: your body, your reputation, your wealth, your health, your children, the outcome of events, the past, the future, the weather, and the world.

Most suffering begins when this boundary is forgotten.

Epictetus warned:

You are disturbed not by events, but by your judgments about them.

Seneca wrote:

A wise man is content with what is his. For what is truly his can never be taken.

Trying to control what isn't yours will break you. Neglecting what is yours will hollow you.

The discipline lies in knowing the difference—and then acting accordingly.

What *Is* Stoic

- Knowing the line between control and concern
- Letting go of outcomes while choosing right action
- Directing energy toward your own mind and choices
- Judging success by alignment, not result

What Is *Not* Stoic

- Chasing outcomes you cannot command
- Letting other people's opinions define you
- Confusing passivity with acceptance
- Surrendering responsibility by calling it "fate"

Go to the Source:

- *Epictetus, Enchiridion §1–2; Discourses I.1*
- *Seneca, Letters 9, 19, 78*
- *Marcus Aurelius, Meditations IV.3, V.20, VI.41*

Field Notes:

⇒ You own your reason. That's enough.

⇒ Do not confuse possession with control.

⇒ Peace begins at the border between what is yours and what is not.

2. Looking for Meaning

On purpose, Logos, and participating nobly

"Everything suits me that suits your designs, O Universe. Nothing is too early or too late if I am in harmony with you."
—Marcus Aurelius

Why am I here? What is this for?
When pain comes, or joy fades, or success feels hollow, the question rises. The Stoics did not ignore it. They faced it—not with abstract metaphysics, but with grounded reverence for **order, reason, and participation**.

Epictetus taught that the Logos—the rational principle that governs all things—moves with purpose, and the task of the individual is not to rewrite the world but to live **in accordance with it**.

Seneca called it *Nature*. He said meaning is not given to you—it is discovered through **how you live**, not what you claim to believe.

And Marcus, surrounded by death and deceit, still wrote:

> *If the gods have taken thought for me, then all is well. If they have not... then why live in a universe void of order?*

Either way, he chose **dignity.**

33

Meaning, to the Stoic, is not assigned. It is **forged**—through reason, virtue, and living as if the whole depends on the part doing its role well.

What *Is* Stoic

- Trusting that a greater order exists, even if unclear
- Seeking meaning through action, not abstraction
- Aligning your life with reason and nature
- Participating nobly, regardless of outcome

What Is *Not* Stoic

- Demanding that the universe explain itself
- Searching for meaning only in personal success
- Mistaking despair for wisdom
- Avoiding engagement because life feels uncertain

Go to the Source:

- *Marcus Aurelius, Meditations II.3, IV.23, V.10, VI.44*
- *Epictetus, Discourses I.6, II.8; Enchiridion §1, §17*
- *Seneca, Letters 16, 41, 65*

Field Notes:

⇒ Meaning is not found in talk. It is found in participation.

⇒ The world may not explain itself. Live as though it speaks.

⇒ If you must ask what it all means—ask while doing good.

3. Facing Fear

On imagined suffering and reclaiming the present

"He suffers more than necessary, who suffers before it is necessary."

—Seneca

Fear is the rehearsal of pain. It projects suffering into the future and invites you to live it now—again and again. The Stoics knew fear well, but they refused to let it command their lives.

Marcus Aurelius reminded himself: *"You have power over your mind—not outside events. Realize this, and you will find strength."*

Fear often arises from **confusing what is not yours for what is**. You fear losing status, control, health, or love—as if they were ever truly yours to keep. But the Stoic doesn't extinguish fear through willpower alone. They **dissolve it by clarity**.

Epictetus asked:

What is to be feared? That which is not up to you? Then it is no concern. That which is? Then you have nothing to fear.

Seneca, facing exile and political execution, wrote of fear as a false prophet. The imagined threat is always worse than what actually comes.

The Stoic does not pretend to be unafraid. But they refuse to **live ruled by shadows**.

What *Is* Stoic

- Preparing the mind without rehearsing suffering
- Accepting danger without surrendering judgment
- Facing the unknown with steadiness, not denial
- Returning to reason when fear tempts reaction

What Is *Not* Stoic

- Worrying about things not yet real
- Letting imagined futures dictate present choices
- Believing that fear itself is proof of danger
- Equating anxiety with moral awareness

Go to the Source:

- *Seneca, Letters 13, 24, 78*
- *Epictetus, Discourses II.1; Enchiridion §5, §12*
- *Marcus Aurelius, Meditations IV.3, VII.2, IX.37*

Field Notes:

⇒ Fear is a lie told by the imagination to the untrained mind.

⇒ Prepare for difficulty, but do not rehearse ruin.

⇒ When in doubt, return to what is yours.

4. Temptation

"Freedom is not achieved by satisfying desire, but by eliminating it."

—Epictetus

Temptation is the seduction of the mind toward what is easy, pleasant, or praised. It disguises itself as fulfillment, but always demands a price: your clarity.

To the Stoic, the danger is not in pleasure—but in becoming **dependent on it.** Comfort is not evil. But once you believe you *need* it, you are no longer free.

Seneca warned:

> *The wise man does not chase pleasure, but does not flee it either. He lets it come and go as the sea breeze.*

Epictetus was sharper:

> **Desire is the chain.** The more you pursue, the less you own yourself.

And Marcus Aurelius, surrounded by luxury, wrote bluntly:

> *Is this what you were made for? To curl up in pleasure? To lick sweet syrup and forget the work of a man?*

41

Temptation is not just about indulgence. It is the pull to lower your aim—to make peace with less than virtue, just because it feels good now.

What *Is* Stoic

- Resisting pleasure that undermines freedom
- Choosing discipline over indulgence
- Recognizing desire as a test, not a guide
- Acting from reason, not appetite

What Is *Not* Stoic

- Seeking comfort as a substitute for peace
- Justifying vice with the excuse of being "natural"
- Equating pleasure with happiness
- Believing self-denial alone is virtue

Go to the Source:

- *Epictetus, Enchiridion §14, §15, §33; Discourses II.23*
- *Seneca, Letters 18, 23, 59*
- *Marcus Aurelius, Meditations V.1, VI.16, IX.4*

Field Notes:

⇒ Not everything pleasant is worth your freedom.

⇒ The path of reason is not paved with avoidance, but with mastery.

⇒ Choose what strengthens the soul, not what flatters the body.

5. Duty

On role, responsibility, and doing what is yours

"If it is not right, do not do it. If it is not true, do not say it."
—Marcus Aurelius

To the Stoic, duty is not assigned by society or status—it arises from **nature itself**. The moment you are born into the world, you are part of it. You owe something to it.

Seneca taught that life is not something to be consumed, but to be **contributed to**. Every role— child, parent, worker, citizen—is an opportunity for virtue to be tested and proven.

No one is born for himself alone," he wrote. *"You are part of a great whole.*

Epictetus reminded that duty is not always dramatic. It may be rising in the morning without complaint, or restraining an angry word.

Don't seek greatness," he said. *"Do what is yours to do.*

Marcus Aurelius returned to this theme constantly. The emperor wrote to himself:

Do not waste time wondering if something is difficult. If it is assigned to you, it is meant for you.

Duty is not about being noticed. It is about being
rightly aligned—with reason, with purpose, with the
moment.

What *Is* Stoic

- Fulfilling your role with integrity
- Treating responsibility as practice, not burden
- Acting justly without waiting for praise
- Doing the work that is yours, without
  complaint

What Is *Not* Stoic

- Resenting obligation while still performing it
- Seeking recognition before taking action
- Using "it's not my job" to escape what is right
- Believing that virtue requires approval

Go to the Source:

- *Marcus Aurelius, Meditations V.1, VI.22, VIII.12*
- *Epictetus, Discourses I.2, II.10; Enchiridion §30*
- *Seneca, Letters 5, 37, 95*

5. Duty

Field Notes:

⇒ Duty is the discipline of the present moment.

⇒ You are not responsible for everything—but you are responsible for something.

⇒ Begin where you stand.

6. The World in Tumult

"Be like the rocky headland on which the waves constantly break. It stands firm, and around it the seething waters are laid to rest."

—Marcus Aurelius

The world is loud, restless, and full of outrage. Corruption spreads. Injustice multiplies. Fools are rewarded. The wrong people are elevated, and the right ones ignored.

The Stoics were not naïve to this. They lived through plagues, wars, assassinations, and the collapse of empires. Marcus led armies through a dying Rome. Seneca walked the palace halls of a mad emperor. Epictetus taught under surveillance, having once lived as property.

Yet none of them believed that the condition of the world should determine the condition of the soul.

"The more you are buffeted by circumstances," Seneca wrote, *"the more you must anchor yourself in reason."*

Anger at the world is not strength. Cynicism is not clarity. The Stoic returns always to what can be governed—*the inner citadel,* as Marcus called it. Not a retreat from the world, but a position within it that cannot be moved.

Epictetus asked:

"Can you be angry with someone who throws dust in your eyes? Wouldn't you simply wash it out?"

Let the world rage. Stand where you are, and do what is yours to do.

What *Is* Stoic

- Guarding your inner clarity amid external chaos
- Responding to disorder with steady character
- Accepting injustice without imitating it
- Remaining useful without being consumed

What Is *Not* Stoic

- Raging at what cannot be controlled
- Withdrawing in bitterness or superiority
- Letting public madness define private peace
- Mistaking cynicism for wisdom

Go to the Source:

- *Marcus Aurelius, Meditations IV.49, V.16, VI.30*
- *Epictetus, Discourses I.1, III.22*
- *Seneca, Letters 5, 28, 73*

Field Notes:

⇒ You were not made to bend with every gust of madness.

⇒ Do not borrow disorder just because others carry it.

⇒ The world will not become calm—but you can.

7. Holding the Flame of Anger

"The best revenge is to be unlike him who did the injury."
—Marcus Aurelius

Anger feels righteous. It surges in like purpose—quick, hot, and heavy. But the Stoics saw it differently. To them, anger was a **mistake of perception**, a fire that consumes more than it corrects.

Seneca warned that *no emotion is more eager for power yet less fit to wield it.* Anger, once embraced, becomes a tyrant. It turns judgment into impulse, and justice into vengeance.

Epictetus asked:

> *What hurts you—being insulted, or believing you must be hurt by it?*

He reminded students: others can provoke, but only **you** can permit the burn.

And Marcus, who surely dealt with more betrayal than most, reminded himself:

> *Does the sun try to do harm? No. It shines. Does the fig tree bear fruit in anger? No. It simply does its work.*

The Stoic doesn't ignore offense. But instead of striking back, they return inward—to the citadel of reason, to the quiet strength that needs no spectacle.

What *Is* Stoic

- Pausing before judgment becomes reaction
- Choosing restraint over retaliation
- Seeing insult as a test of clarity
- Keeping peace within, even in conflict

What Is *Not* Stoic

- Justifying cruelty in the name of justice
- Confusing silence with agreement
- Believing that anger proves conviction
- Using offense as an excuse to abandon virtue

Go to the Source:

- *Seneca, On Anger (De Ira), Books I–III*
- *Epictetus, Discourses II.18, Enchiridion §20*
- *Marcus Aurelius, Meditations VI.6, XI.18, XII.18*

Field Notes:

⇒ Anger is a thief. It takes clarity, then character.

⇒ Pause. Ask: *Is this mine to carry?*

⇒ Justice is not louder than wrath—it is stronger in silence.

8. Letting Go

On loss, transience and returning to what is

"Never say about anything, 'I have lost it,' but rather, 'I have given it back.'"

—Epictetus

Loss is not just an event—it is a confrontation with **attachment**. Something loved, valued, or trusted has slipped beyond reach, and the mind panics at the gap it leaves behind.

The Stoics knew this ache well. But they taught that the pain of loss is sharpened by illusion—the illusion that what was never truly yours could somehow be held forever.

Seneca reminded that everything we love is *"on loan."* He wrote:

You must behave as if you had lost them, not as if they were yours.

Epictetus taught students to rehearse letting go—not to harden the heart, but to soften the blow. To see clearly that **what is not yours cannot be stolen.**

Even Marcus, writing through grief, counseled himself not to ask *why* something was taken, but to ask *what remains to be done now, with virtue.*

57

Letting go, for the Stoic, is not a surrender. It is a return—to what is yours, and nothing more.

What *Is* Stoic

- Accepting loss as part of nature's rhythm
- Grieving without collapse
- Releasing attachment to outcomes beyond your control
- Holding love without the illusion of permanence

What Is *Not* Stoic

- Suppressing sorrow out of pride
- Pretending indifference to protect ego
- Claiming "nothing matters" as a defense
- Denying the emotional cost of letting go

Go to the Source:

- *Epictetus, Enchiridion §11, §14, §33*
- *Seneca, Letter 98; On Consolation to Marcia*
- *Marcus Aurelius, Meditations IV.23, VII.50, VIII.46*

Field Notes:

⇒ You were given much. And nothing was promised.

⇒ Grief is natural. Clinging is not.

⇒ Return to the present. It is all you are owed.

9. Falling and Returning

On failure, humility, and the power of beginning again

"When jarred, unavoidably, by circumstance, return at once to yourself, and don't stay outside your own soul."
—Marcus Aurelius

Everyone falls. The Stoics never denied this. Even the wise man stumbles—into frustration, weakness, foolishness, even shame. But the difference is in the return.

Falling is not failure. **Remaining fallen is.**

Epictetus reminded:

When you blunder, do not dwell on the failure. Instead, pick yourself up and say: 'I will begin again, this time with more care.'

Marcus wrote *Meditations* not as a performance of virtue, but as a tool for returning to it. Each page is a quiet admission: *I lost my footing. Now I begin again.*

There is no Stoic requirement to be unshakable. Only to return—to reason, to clarity, to discipline—again and again. Each return is a small proof that freedom still lives in you.

What *Is* Stoic

- Admitting failure without surrendering to it
- Returning to reason as often as needed
- Treating setbacks as part of the path
- Beginning again without shame

What Is *Not* Stoic

- Believing one mistake erases your progress
- Using imperfection as permission to drift
- Turning guilt into identity
- Waiting for ideal conditions before trying again

Go to the Source:

- *Marcus Aurelius, Meditations VI.11, VI.26, VIII.1*
- *Epictetus, Enchiridion §10, §53; Discourses I.4*
- *Seneca, Letters 13, 35, 110*

Field Notes:

⇒ The fall is not the danger. The drift is.

⇒ Begin again. Not later. Now.

⇒ Each return is a rehearsal for the final one.

10. Dignity

On posture, quiet strength, and bearing oneself rightly

"Look within. Within is the fountain of good, and it will ever bubble up, if you will ever dig."
—Marcus Aurelius

Dignity is not something others give you. It is the **way you carry yourself**—especially when no one is watching.

To the Stoic, it is the quiet expression of alignment between thought and action. It does not swagger, and it does not shrink. It walks straight, even under burden.

Seneca wrote:

> *The wise man is content with himself. He walks with his head held high—not with arrogance, but with assurance.*

Epictetus warned that those who seek admiration will always be someone else's servant. True dignity, he said, is born from **freedom from needing praise**.

Marcus Aurelius returned often to the idea of **nobility in thought**—to let the mind govern the body, to act not from mood but from principle.

"Conduct every act of your life as though it were your last," he wrote—not in panic, but in **nobility**.

65

Dignity is the tone of a well-ordered life. Not perfect. Not loud. Just steady.

What *Is* Stoic

- Standing with calm confidence, not arrogance
- Living in alignment with your principles
- Speaking and acting with restraint and clarity
- Letting conduct reveal character

What Is *Not* Stoic

- Demanding respect to feel worthy
- Using Stoicism to mask insecurity
- Seeking approval through moral posturing
- Mistaking silence for superiority

Go to the Source:

- *Marcus Aurelius, Meditations II.5, III.6, V.1, VI.30*
- *Epictetus, Enchiridion §13, §29; Discourses I.19*
- *Seneca, Letters 66, 71, 80*

Field Notes:

⇒ Dignity does not need applause.

⇒ Stand in a way that reflects what you believe.

⇒ When in doubt, choose what honors your own soul.

11. Tasting Victory without Swallowing It

"It is not the man who has too little, but the man who craves more, who is poor."
—Seneca

Success is seductive. It flatters the ego, inflates the self, and tempts a man to believe he is the cause of all good things. But the Stoics warned: **fortune is not virtue.** It arrives and departs as it pleases.

To enjoy success without being owned by it is rare. The Stoic does not refuse joy—but refuses to become drunk on it.

Marcus wrote:

Receive without pride. Let it go without grief.

Epictetus asked:

If a ship you command sails well, do you think yourself a god? Or do you credit the sea and the weather?

Seneca knew glory intimately—and saw its dangers up close. He taught that external success means little unless the **inner judgment remains stable.** One must taste victory, not swallow it whole.

To walk with honor through success is not to deny it—but to carry it lightly. As a tool, not a trophy.

What *Is* Stoic

- Enjoying success without being ruled by it
- Accepting praise without craving more
- Remaining steady when things go well
- Remembering that fortune is not virtue

What Is *Not* Stoic

- Measuring worth by recognition or results
- Letting accomplishment inflate identity
- Chasing validation after the task is done
- Believing success confirms moral goodness

Go to the Source:

- *Seneca, Letters 9, 74, 110*
- *Epictetus, Discourses I.1, III.13*
- *Marcus Aurelius, Meditations IV.3, V.20, VI.30*

Field Notes:

⇒ Success is not proof of character.

⇒ Character is shown in how success is carried.

⇒ Celebrate without attachment.

⇒ Leave the party without clinging to the applause.

12. Reputation

On praise, judgment, and freedom from performance

"If you seek tranquility, do less. Or more precisely, do what's essential. Which brings a double satisfaction: to do less, and to do it well. Most of what we say and do is not essential. Ask yourself at every moment: Is this necessary?"

—Marcus Aurelius

The desire for recognition is natural—but it is also dangerous. The Stoics warned that **reputation is a shifting wind**, and those who live for it are never truly at rest.

Epictetus was blunt:

If you want to be free, disregard what others think of you.

Seneca, too, saw the peril: fame makes people behave not as they are, but as they are expected to be.

"What matters," he wrote, *"is not what people say of you, but what you say to yourself."*

Marcus Aurelius, emperor of Rome, reminded himself that reputation is hollow. That even the most admired will be forgotten. That pleasing the crowd is a poor substitute for inner alignment.

Soon you will have forgotten all things. And soon all things will have forgotten you.

Reputation fades. The soul remains. The Stoic chooses to be whole, not popular.

What *Is* Stoic

- Valuing your character above your image
- Living by principle, not perception
- Accepting misunderstanding without distress
- Letting the judgment that matters be your own

What Is *Not* Stoic

- Shaping yourself to win approval
- Fearing criticism more than wrongdoing
- Performing virtue for an audience
- Believing praise is proof of truth

Go to the Source:

- *Marcus Aurelius, Meditations IV.3, VI.30, VII.31*
- *Epictetus, Discourses I.21, III.1; Enchiridion §1, §33*
- *Seneca, Letters 5, 9, 94*

Field Notes:

⇒ If others misunderstand you, be glad: they cannot steal your virtue.

⇒ You are not what they say—you are what you choose.

⇒ Live with substance, not performance.

13. Truthfulness

On clarity, speech, and inner alignment

"If it is not true, do not say it. If it is not right, do not do it."
—Marcus Aurelius

Truthfulness is not just about what is said. It is about how one **lives**—without illusion, without performance, and without disguising one's own motives.

The Stoics held truth as sacred—not because it pleased others, but because it preserved **inner alignment**. To lie, even slightly, is to **fracture the soul**.

Epictetus reminded:

If you tell yourself a lie long enough, you become its slave.

Seneca warned against flattering others or masking discomfort with false words. He wrote:

Say what you believe. Speak not to please, but to express.

Marcus Aurelius returned to truth often. He urged himself to **strip away pretense**—to speak and act as a philosopher, not as an emperor.

"Let your words be simple and direct," he wrote, *"and let your purpose be clear."*

Truthfulness is not aggression. It is the quiet discipline of not betraying the logos within you, even to smooth a conversation.

What *Is* Stoic

- Speaking plainly, with purpose and restraint
- Living without disguise or distortion
- Aligning words with actions
- Honoring truth even when it's inconvenient

What Is *Not* Stoic

- Bending the truth to avoid discomfort
- Using flattery to gain favor
- Equating bluntness with virtue
- Believing silence excuses dishonesty

Go to the Source:

- *Marcus Aurelius, Meditations IV.24, VI.30, VIII.5*
- *Epictetus, Enchiridion §33; Discourses II.12*
- *Seneca, Letters 3, 10, 79*

Field Notes:

⇒ Speak plainly. Deceit poisons slowly.

⇒ The truth is not always easy—but it is always lighter to carry.

⇒ Your words are a mirror. Keep them clean.

14. In the Stillness

On solitude, reflection, and the unshaken soul

"Nowhere can a man find a quieter or more untroubled retreat than in his own soul."

—Marcus Aurelius

The world demands movement. Achievement. Noise. But the Stoics understood the power of **stillness**— not inactivity, but presence. A place where the mind can return to itself and remember what matters.

Stillness is not withdrawal from duty. It is the soil in which right action grows.

Seneca wrote:

The mind must be allowed some time to recover, to dwell with itself.

Epictetus reminded that a man who cannot sit in quiet reflection has not yet trained his freedom. He is still a slave to distraction.

And Marcus, wearied by war and politics, found in his evening meditations a kind of retreat—**a return to the inner citadel**, where no empire, no enemy, no illness could reach.

Stillness is not escape. It is **readiness**—the clearing of the fog before the next step is taken.

What *Is* Stoic

- Seeking quiet to examine your own thoughts
- Using solitude as a place of strength
- Letting stillness restore judgment
- Returning inward without escaping the world

What Is *Not* Stoic

- Avoiding people to avoid effort
- Confusing withdrawal with peace
- Using isolation as a shield
- Mistaking stillness for inaction

Go to the Source:

- *Marcus Aurelius, Meditations IV.3, VI.7, VIII.48*
- *Seneca, On Tranquility of Mind; Letters 2, 28, 56*
- *Epictetus, Discourses I.6, II.22*

Field Notes:

⇒ If you cannot sit in silence, you are not yet free.

⇒ Noise is not life. Stillness is not death.

⇒ Return to your soul. That is your shelter.

15. Among the Living

On enduring others with patience and integrity

"Whenever you are offended at someone's fault, turn to yourself and ask: Do I not have the same fault?"

—Marcus Aurelius

People are messy. They interrupt, disappoint, insult, fail, and fall short. And still—we live among them.

The Stoic does not retreat from others. Nor does he demand their perfection. He accepts that **to live is to be among flawed humans**, and that the only proper control lies within his own response.

Epictetus reminded:

We have two ears and one mouth so that we may listen twice as much as we speak.

Seneca advised choosing friends not for agreement, but for strength of character. He warned that anger, gossip, and envy were the illnesses of those who lived **outside themselves**.

And Marcus, emperor of all Rome, wrote endlessly to himself not about governance—but about **patience**. About forgiveness. About remembering that the man who offends is *just like you*, and often acting out of ignorance, not malice.

The Stoic lives among others not with resignation—
but with **resolve**: to be just, kind, and unshaken by
the tempers of the crowd.

What *Is* Stoic

- Responding to others with patience and clarity
- Treating people as fellow travelers, not
  obstacles
- Choosing your company with intention
- Practicing virtue in relationship, not just in
  solitude

What Is *Not* Stoic

- Expecting others to live by your standards
- Withdrawing in contempt or frustration
- Using philosophy as an excuse for coldness
- Believing peace requires isolation

15. *Among the Living*

Go to the Source:

- *Marcus Aurelius, Meditations II.1, VI.26, IX.42*
- *Seneca, Letters 11, 53, 88*
- *Epictetus, Discourses I.6, I.18; Enchiridion §42*

Field Notes:

⇒ Others are not yours to correct, only to understand.

⇒ Walk with people, not above them.

⇒ If insulted, consider: *Have I done the same?*

16. Friendship

On shared virtue, chosen companions, and right closeness

"Associate with those who will make a better man of you. Welcome those whom you yourself can improve."

—Seneca

The Stoic does not withdraw from others—but they choose carefully. Friendship is not flattery or escape. It is a **mutual sharpening** of soul and reason.

Seneca held that true friendship is formed not from shared pleasures, but from shared values.

"I do not aim to be the friend of many," he wrote, *"but of one to whom I may be of help, and who may help me."*

Epictetus warned against dependence disguised as affection. He taught that if friendship becomes a trap, it is no longer noble—it is a **soft chain**.

And Marcus Aurelius, while often alone, found strength in companions who reminded him of the Logos in daily life. His reflections show that the **best friend is one who helps you return to yourself.**

The Stoic chooses friends as one might choose a co-pilot: not for entertainment, but for truth and endurance.

What *Is* Stoic

- Choosing friends who strengthen your character
- Giving and receiving truth without flattery
- Valuing shared virtue over shared opinion
- Remaining loyal without dependence

What Is *Not* Stoic

- Using friendship for validation or comfort
- Avoiding honest speech to preserve harmony
- Binding your peace to another's approval
- Mistaking closeness for possession

Go to the Source:

- *Seneca, Letters 3, 9, 35, 63*
- *Epictetus, Discourses II.22, III.24*
- *Marcus Aurelius, Meditations I.6, I.17, VI.12*

Field Notes:

⇒ Choose friends who make you stronger—and demand the same in return.

⇒ A friend is not one who agrees, but one who aligns.

⇒ Affection is not weakness. It is trust practiced with discernment.

17. The Body Borrowed: Illness & Aging

On suffering, impermanence, and the body as station

"You are a little soul carrying around a corpse."
—Epictetus

When the body weakens—whether from sickness, age, or fatigue—the illusion of ownership begins to fail. The Stoics never pretended the body didn't matter. But they were clear: **you are not your body**. It is not your enemy. It is not your identity. It is your station.

Pain is not moral. Disease is not failure. Decay is not defeat. These things happen to everyone. The Stoic difference is how one carries the weight.

Seneca wrote that the wise person endures illness *"as he endures a journey—without complaint, if possible."*

Epictetus taught students to say not *"I am sick"* but *"My body is sick."*
A subtle shift. But one that returns control to the mind.

Marcus Aurelius, likely dying as he wrote, reminded himself that "what harms the vessel does not harm the soul."

To the Stoic, suffering is real. But **how you meet it** is still your choice. The body may bend, but the will remains yours to govern.

What *Is* Stoic

- Caring for the body without identifying with it
- Enduring pain without self-pity
- Accepting aging as part of nature's rhythm
- Letting illness refine the soul, not diminish it

What Is *Not* Stoic

- Defining yourself by your strength or health
- Resisting what time or nature has made inevitable
- Believing suffering erases dignity
- Treating decline as failure

17. The Body Borrowed:
Illness & Aging

Go to the Source:

- *Epictetus, Enchiridion §9 and Discourses I.1*
- *Seneca, Letter 78 (On the Healing of the Soul)*
- *Marcus Aurelius, Meditations II.6, VI.30, IX.4*

Field Notes:

⇒ You are not your flesh. You are what chooses how to bear it.

⇒ Pain is not punishment. Aging is not failure.

⇒ The soul governs. The body carries.

18. Approaching the End

On death, readiness, and returning without fear

"It is not death that a man should fear, but never beginning to live."

—Marcus Aurelius

Death is the boundary no one escapes. But the Stoics did not dread it. They studied it. Rehearsed it. Spoke of it without euphemism. Not to morbidly obsess— but to live without illusion.

Epictetus told his students:

You are a mortal. You have been given a body for a time, and it will be taken. Act accordingly.

Seneca wrote his essays knowing Nero could order his death at any moment. He called each day a rehearsal. Each breath, a gift returned.

"Life is long if you know how to use it," he wrote. *"But the man who lives in fear of death never really lives at all."*

And Marcus, nearing the end of his life, reminded himself that all he was would soon be dust—and yet, **the Logos remains.** The way, the order, the virtue—that is what matters. That is what endures.

The Stoic meets death not with bravado, but with
readiness. Not defiance, but peace. For death is not
an error. It is a return.

What *Is* Stoic

- Facing death as a natural part of life
- Preparing the soul rather than fearing the
  body's end
- Letting mortality clarify what matters
- Meeting the end with readiness, not resistance

What Is *Not* Stoic

- Treating death as an error or injustice
- Postponing life out of fear of its end
- Believing that to die is to be defeated
- Clinging to what was never promised

Go to the Source:

- Marcus Aurelius, Meditations II.11, VI.28,
  XII.36
- Epictetus, Enchiridion §7, §11, §51
- Seneca, On the Shortness of Life; Letters 24,
  70, 77

Field Notes:

⇒ You were never promised a length of days—only this one.

⇒ Fear of death is fear of nature. And nature does not err.

⇒ Begin to live now. The end is not later. The end is *always* near.

19. When You Must Choose

On decisive action, freedom, and stepping forward

"You may be unconquerable, if you enter into no contest in which it is not in your power to conquer."
   —Epictetus

There comes a moment—quiet or violent—when clarity must become choice. Not theory. Not intention. Action. The Stoics placed supreme value on this: the moment when the mind must decide, and **the rest of life bends around it.**

Seneca warned against drifting through days without deciding who you are.

"If a man knows not to which port he sails," he wrote, *"no wind is favorable."*

Epictetus reminded that we are not animals, bound to instinct. We are moral beings—capable of **deliberation, judgment, and resolve.** But to delay the moment of choice is to live at the mercy of other people's purposes.

Marcus Aurelius, in the middle of campaign and collapse, wrote:

No longer talk about what the good man is like. Be one.

You cannot always choose your circumstances. But you always choose how to meet them. And in that choice—repeated, tested, embodied—you become what you are.

What *Is* Stoic

- Acting from reason, not impulse
- Accepting uncertainty without paralysis
- Choosing what aligns with virtue, not convenience
- Owning the consequences of your decision

What Is *Not* Stoic

- Delaying choice to avoid discomfort
- Looking outward for moral permission
- Letting fear or desire cloud judgment
- Believing indecision is safer than error

Go to the Source:

- *Epictetus, Enchiridion §1, §29, §53; Discourses II.2*
- *Seneca, Letters 71, 120; On the Firmness of the Wise Man*
- *Marcus Aurelius, Meditations II.5, III.1, X.31*

Field Notes:

⇒ Choice is the practice of freedom. Use it.

⇒ Delay is surrender. Decisiveness is dignity.

⇒ You shape the world more in one act than in a thousand thoughts.

20. Clear Conscience

On judgment, peace of mind, and living clean

"A good character, when tested, holds firm. A bad one collapses under its own weight."

—Epictetus

Conscience, to the Stoic, is not guilt—it is **alignment**. A mind in harmony with reason does not tremble. It does not boast. It stands firm, because there is nothing hidden.

Seneca wrote:

What need is there to seek refuge from the judgment of others, when you live in such a way that you fear your own?

Epictetus taught that **self-scrutiny is the root of freedom**. One must examine one's motives as a craftsman examines tools—honestly, constantly, and without excuse.

Marcus Aurelius reflected nightly not on what others had done wrong, but on **whether he himself had lived by the logos**. Did he act from justice? Did he speak from clarity? Did he waste the day?

A clear conscience is not perfection—it is the refusal to lie to oneself. And in that refusal, the soul becomes still.

What *Is* Stoic

- Living so that your own judgment is enough
- Examining motives as carefully as actions
- Letting peace come from alignment, not approval
- Correcting yourself without self-condemnation

What Is *Not* Stoic

- Hiding behind technical correctness while betraying intention
- Confusing guilt with morality
- Seeking peace through others' validation
- Using Stoicism to avoid accountability

Go to the Source:

- *Epictetus, Discourses I.4, II.11; Enchiridion §33, §47*
- *Seneca, Letters 13, 43, 83*
- *Marcus Aurelius, Meditations III.10, IV.3, VI.30*

Field Notes:

⇒   If you need to hide it, it's already broken you.

⇒   The judgment that matters most is your own.

⇒   Peace of mind is not a gift. It is a habit.

21. Time

"You act like mortals in all that you fear, and like immortals in all that you desire."

—Seneca

Time is not a resource—it is **your life**. The Stoics warned that most people fear death while wasting the very thing they claim to treasure.

Seneca opens *On the Shortness of Life* with a blow:

> *"It is not that we have a short time to live, but that we waste much of it."*

Epictetus said that nothing is more foolish than postponing what matters. Each delay is a betrayal of reason.

> *"How long will you wait,"* he asked, *"before you demand the best of yourself?"*

Marcus Aurelius returned to the theme again and again: everything changes, dissolves, disappears. What matters is how you used your brief flicker of breath.

> *"Concentrate every minute like a man,"* he wrote, *"on doing what's in front of you with precision and purpose."*

Time is not yours to hold. But it is yours to **honor**.

What *Is* Stoic

- Honoring the present as your only certainty
- Spending time as if it belongs to virtue
- Remembering that delay is not neutral—it is surrender
- Living now, not someday

What Is *Not* Stoic

- Postponing growth until conditions are perfect
- Wasting time while fearing death
- Mistaking busyness for purpose
- Acting as if time can be stored or reclaimed

Go to the Source:

- *Seneca, On the Shortness of Life; Letters 1, 49, 101*
- *Marcus Aurelius, Meditations II.14, IV.3, V.16, VI.15*
- *Epictetus, Enchiridion §1, §17; Discourses I.1*

Field Notes:

⇒ You cannot bargain with time. You can only spend it.

⇒ Delay is a quiet form of surrender.

⇒ Begin now. There is no other moment.

Author's Note

This work was written as a collaboration between a human author and an advanced AI writing partner.

It was not our aim to modernize the Stoics, nor to impersonate them. Instead, the goal was to step aside and let their voices speak again—clearly, without clutter. The reflections you've just read were not invented, but drawn carefully from the original texts of Zeno's lineage, with the hope that they might serve as a compass, not a conclusion.

This is not a system. It is a guide.
Not a doctrine, but a conversation.
Not a performance—but a return.

If the work helped you walk the Porch with steadier footing, it has done its part.

—WJS

www.ingramcontent.com/pod-product-compliance
Lightning Source LLC
Chambersburg PA
CBHW032039040426
42449CB00007B/950